# The
# Prentice Hall
# Writer's Journal

PEARSON

Prentice
Hall

Upper Saddle River, New Jersey 07458

© 2005 by PEARSON EDUCATION, INC.
Upper Saddle River, New Jersey 07458

10 9 8 7 6 5 4 3 2 1

ISBN 0–13–184900–X

Printed in the United States of America

# A Note to Journal Writers

## What is a journal?

A journal—a series of thoughtful writings a person creates—can be many things. For example, scribbling not-to-be forgotten thoughts, phrases, and feelings on scraps of paper can be a writer's sourcebook of ideas. A counseling patient's compilation of clippings, photographs, and emotional outpourings can be a tool for self-analysis. A young adult's lock-and-key diary of daily events and dreams can be a way to study life's changes.

But one element of keeping a journal doesn't vary: journal writers recognize the value of writing as a critical ingredient in helping us articulate connections between what we know, or think we know, and the new information that bombards us daily.

Journaling, critically reflecting on our thoughts, ideas, awareness of issues, and feelings, is a tool to help us gain an understanding of ourselves. It can help us discover wisdom we already possess, encourage us to reevaluate our thinking, and cause us to clarify long-held beliefs. Journaling can aid our memory, document our learning, and force us to raise questions we need to answer.

As writer Joseph Epstein says, "A journal provides one with that best of audiences, that most loyal supporter, that closest and most understanding and greatest good-hearted of friends — oneself." In other words, a journal entry is a conversation with yourself. This holds true even if others, like your professor, eavesdrop on the conversation.

## Writing in this Journal

While it is important to understand that there is no wrong way to journal, it is equally important to understand that the physical act of writing in a journal does not automatically ensure critical reflection or other learning outcomes. If your journal writing is to be beneficial, it must be purposeful.

What you write can go in any direction you want: somewhere that is safe and secure or somewhere that you've never been before. For example, you can cheer the author's insight, yell at the author's lack of understanding, philosophize, ask questions, give examples from your life that support the author's thought, or provide a story that weakens the author's premise. You can decide you want to read about the topic or the author before you comment. You even tell why a prompt has no meaning to you and have a different conversation.

I encourage you to establish a routine for journal writing, but do not make it into a mechanical chore. It should be your time to deliberate, reflect, and consider possibilities. I also recommend that you to experiment with various styles. Write an entry as a letter to a friend, author, or politician. Write a dialog between yourself and an author whose work you've recently read. Write a *Saturday Night Live* skit, an argumentative essay, or simply free-write.

Your professor will let you know how your journal will be used. For example, whether it is for personal use only or to generate material for other assignments, and whether it will be graded for writing style, grammar, content, and/or number of entries.

## Where can you find more information on journaling?

As there is for most endeavors, a wealth of information and advice is available on "how to journal." If you would like more background on journaling, ask your professors and learning-center staff, examine one of the numerous books on the subject, or explore one of these websites.

www.journalforyou.com/
www.writingthejourney.com/
www.journal-writing.com/

Read, think, write, enjoy!
Jane McGrath
Prentice Hall Author

*A good time to keep your mouth shut is when you're in deep water.*

—Sidney Goff

*A great many people think they are thinking when they are merely rearranging their prejudices.*

—WILLIAM JAMES

*A man's feet should be planted in his country, but his eyes should survey the world.*

—George Santayana

*A mind once stretched by a new idea never regains its original dimensions.*

—ANONYMOUS

*A new idea is delicate. It can be killed by a sneer or a yawn; it can be stabbed to death by a joke or worried to death by a frown on the right person's brow.*

—Charles Brower

*For success, attitude is equally as important as ability.*

—HARRY F. BANKS

*Always be a first-rate version of yourself, instead of a second-rate version of somebody else.*

—JUDY GARLAND

*The right to be heard does not automatically include the right to be taken seriously.*

—HUBERT H. HUMPHREY

*If you aren't fired with enthusiasm, you will be fired with enthusiasm.*

—VINCE LOMBARDI

*It is the true nature of mankind to learn from mistakes, not from example.*

—FRED HOYLE

*There is nothing like returning to a place that remains unchanged to find the ways in which you yourself have altered.*

—Nelson Mandela

*I don't measure a man's success by how high he climbs, but how high he bounces when he hits bottom.*

—General George S. Patton

*If we don't believe in freedom of expression for people we despise, we don't believe in it at all.*

—NOAM CHOMSKY

*A pessimist sees the difficulty in every opportunity; an optimist sees the opportunity in every difficulty.*

—SIR WINSTON CHURCHILL

*It's not that I'm so smart, it's just that I stay with problems longer.*

—ALBERT EINSTEIN

*Heredity deals the cards; environment plays the hand.*

—CHARLES L. BREWER

*The defect of equality is that we only desire it with our superiors.*

—Henry Becque

*The only thing more expensive than education is ignorance.*

—Benjamin Franklin

*Education is our passport to the future, for tomorrow belongs to the people who prepare for it today.*

—MALCOLM X

*Censorship, like charity, should begin at home; but unlike charity, it should end there.*

—CLARE BOOTH LUCE

*A professional is a person who can do his best at a time when he doesn't particularly feel like it.*

—ALISTAIR COOKE

*Teachers open the door, but you must enter by yourself.*

—CHINESE PROVERB

*The real art of conversation is not only to say the right thing at the right place but to leave unsaid the wrong thing at the tempting moment.*

—Dorothy Nevill

*Procrastination is the thief of time.*

—EDWARD YOUNG

*An education is what you remember after you have forgotten everything that you've learned.*

—ALBERT EINSTEIN

*The value of life is computed not by its duration but by its donation.*

—William James

*To read without reflecting is like eating without digesting.*

—EDMUND BURKE

*The highest result of education is tolerance.*

—HELEN KELLER

*Temper gets you in trouble. Pride keeps you there.*

—ANONYMOUS

*I disapprove of what you say, but I will defend to the death your right to say it.*

—VOLTAIRE

*There are all these ideals about what is perfect and what is beautiful and what is smart, but the most appealing thing is, that which is me is nobody else.*

—JENNIFER LOPEZ

*Too many folks go through life running from something that isn't after them.*

—ANONYMOUS

*In the business world, the rearview mirror is always clearer than the windshield.*

—WARREN BUFFETT

*It is the mark of an educated mind to be able to entertain a thought without accepting it.*

—ARISTOTLE

_____

_____

_____

_____

_____

_____

_____

_____

_____

_____

_____

_____

_____

_____

_____

_____

_____

*To reveal ourselves openly and honestly takes the rawest kind of courage.*

—JOHN POWELL